SWINDON RAIL SCENE

HYDRAULICS TO HSTs

Garry Stroud

AMBERLEY

Front Cover – top

Now preserved as part of the National Collection and based at the National Railway museum in York, Western No. D1023 *Western Fusilier*, painted in maroon livery but without name or number plates, stands outside the former test house at Swindon Works in the company of Nos 08080 and 08146 on 22 March 1981.

Front cover – bottom

In its original HST InterCity 125 livery, power car No. 43192, together with No. 43020 on the rear, prepare to depart Swindon station at 13.04 pm with the 12.00 Paddington to Swansea service on 29 October 1985. In the distance the local DMU service to Gloucester awaits departure.

Rear cover

While other members of its class were being scrapped only yards away, North British Class 22 No. D6319 gained fame as the last of its type to receive an overhaul and repaint in Swindon Works. D6319 is seen here in early 1971 under the 'A' shop roof. Ironically, the loco only saw limited use, being sent back to the works during 1972, and by the time the year was out had been reduced to scrap metal.

First published 2020

Amberley Publishing
The Hill, Stroud
Gloucestershire, GL5 4EP

www.amberley-books.com

ISBN 978 1 3981 0054 1 (print)
ISBN 978 1 3981 0055 8 (ebook)

British Library Cataloguing in Publication Data.
A catalogue record for this book is available from the British Library.

Origination by Amberley Publishing.
Printed in the UK.

Introduction

Like most railway towns and workshops that were once part of the UK's railway history, Swindon has, over the years, seen its fair share of change, finally ending when the works hooter sounded for the last time in 1986 and brought an end a legacy of railway construction and repair since the Victorian era. Even now in the twenty-first century it is still evolving with the electrification of the line from Paddington to Bristol/South Wales, together with the completion and reinstatement of the double track section between Swindon and Kemble on the Gloucester line.

Growing up in Swindon it was as if everyone you spoke to or met around the town in the 1950s had some form of connection with the railway or works to some degree or another, such was its employment influence on the area. It was as a teenager in the early 1960s that the elimination of steam on the Western Region, together with the introduction of new Hydraulic motive power, led to numerous visits to the station and works. It was Wednesday afternoons that the works opened its doors to the general public. Many visitors including myself made their way down to the main works entrance, in London Street, to join the ever-increasing number of enthusiasts all eager to see what the mighty 'A' shop had in store. When the works visit was over, I often descended on Swindon station in the late afternoon. Sometimes it seemed (especially on school holidays) there were more spotters on the west end of the station than passengers.

It also became increasingly apparent, as a schoolboy during those visits in the early 60s, that major change was on the way. Following the BR modernisation plan, steam was disappearing fast on the Western Region. Although steam could still be seen in and around the works in ever decreasing numbers, it was rapidly being replaced with new diesel hydraulic motive power. 1962/63 were particularly interesting as we noted down the temporary chalk numbers that were written on the frames of new-build Westerns within the 'A' shop.

British Rail offered me employment following a period as an apprentice. I eventually became an employee within the works as a coach/locomotive painter, working on those very locomotives that not so many years ago I was so eager to see on those Wednesday afternoon works visits.

Not only was I painting these locos, but around the early 1970s that I started photographing them as well. Many a lunchtime was spent recording the locomotives in and around the works site. The 'A' shop and con yard were particular favourites, everything form gleaming ex-works examples to withdrawn locomotives could be seen either awaiting component recovery or the cutter's torch.

Being employed within the works did have its advantages and enabled me to obtain images where the normal visitor would certainly not have been allowed.

Throughout the 1970s more and more locomotives began to arrive, with the con yard and sidings around the works being taken over with ever increasing examples of withdrawn hydraulic motive power. It was the Westerns though that had the most profound effect, attaining an almost cult status in the mid-1970s. Here was the flagship of the hydraulic fleet, which only a few years before I had witnessed being built in the 'A' shop, now being reduced to scrap metal.

Although the scrapping of the hydraulic fleet was bad enough, the works was fast reducing in size as well, with the wrecking ball working overtime in this period to reduce everything to rubble. Going in this decade was the former carriage side workshops, east of the Gloucester line, being replaced by new industrial premises. Even Swindon station was transformed to island status, with the former Down side buildings demolished to make way for a new station frontage at the bottom of another Lego-looking office block.

With Class 50s, 47s and eventually HSTs now being in charge of the Paddington expresses, the 1980s dawned again with a new chapter in the works fortunes, as former Midland locomotives Class 24s, 25s, 40s etc. graced the works yards, either to be scrapped or for storage. The north yard alongside the Gloucester line was the holding sidings for these locomotives. Although the 'A' shop was busy with component recovery on these locomotives, plus still maintaining the Class 08 fleet, it was not to last. Decisions were taken at a higher level that the works would close completely and in 1985, during the GWR 150 celebrations, the announcement was made, bringing to an end not just a piece of railway history but of Swindon's railway heritage.

Today the majority of the works site is now reduced to history, the mighty 'A' shop and con yard having long gone, although the excellent Steam Museum still gives visitors an appreciation of the railway heritage of this once proud site. Also, with the Great Western designer outlet centre situated where a small part of these former workshops once echoed to the sound of railway activity, one can now do your shopping and make purchases on your credit card.

Change, though, is inevitable in life, and railways have been changing since their birth. The photos represented in this book cover two decades, from 1969 through to 1989. They not only cover views of locomotives and DMUs in and around the works, but the station and yards etc., together with main line images towards Stratton St Margaret, in the east, Royal Wootton Bassett, to the west, and Purton on the Gloucester line, to the north – a railway landscape and period in the town's history that is now lost forever.

Garry Stroud

Note: Unless indicated, all photos by the author.

Demolished during 1971, the former Swindon steam shed, situated to the right of the main Gloucester line, has seen better days in this 10 February 1969 photograph. No. D1638, later renumbered to 47054, awaits its next turn of duty outside the shed, while Hymek No. D7030 stands just inside the doors.

Having arrived at the works for mechanical attention, former Western Region Pullman driving car No. W60097 makes for an unusual sight under the 'A' shop roof in this early May 1971 view. Just visible to the right is green livery Class 08 No. D3999.

Photographed from the overhead traverser inside the 'A' shop again during early May 1971, Warship No. D821 *Greyhound* is awaiting primer to be applied following its application of filler, while Hymek No. D7026 stands alongside partly painted in grey undercoat. In the distance can also be seen D6319 undergoing its final overhaul and repaint into BR blue livery.

Another image from the main 'A' shop traverser, taken during early May 1971, although now facing in the opposite direction. Three Westerns are seen in this view, nearest the camera is No. D1047 *Western Lord* in green primer, while No. D1037 *Western Empress* and No. D1050 *Western Ruler* are in various stages of painting into BR blue livery.

Withdrawn North British Class 22 No. D6340 stands at the works reception sidings during the summer of 1971. Although looking in fairly good external condition, this locomotive, together with many of its classmates, ended their days at Swindon's con yard.

A sight all too familiar during the 1970s. Withdrawn and awaiting the cutter's torch at the rear of the 'A' shop stands a line-up of former hydraulic motive power. In faded green livery, No. D6312 keeps company with Nos D6352, D6309, D6307 and Warship No. D864 *Zambesi*, recorded on 2 August 1971.

Withdrawn during June 1971, former Swansea Landore Class 03 shunter No. D2378, still in BR green livery, arrived at Swindon works for scrap. Seen here shortly after arrival on 2 August 1971, the locomotive stands at the rear of the 'A' shop awaiting its fate. By October the following year No. D2378 was just another statistic of the con yard cutting crew.

Being the last of its class to receive a main overhaul at Swindon Works, Warship No. D818 *Glory* looks almost ready for the road in this 2 August 1971 image. It was a short life though, for on 1 November 1972 *Glory* was withdrawn from service. She remained at Plymouth Laira until April 1973 when she again returned to Swindon for intended parts removal.

With its overhaul nearly completed, Hymek No. D7011 awaits final attention before release in this 'A' shop view of 2 August 1971. Withdrawn from Old Oak Common during March 1975, D7011 was one of the last survivors of this class in traffic.

Soon for a date with the scrap man, withdrawn Class 22 No. D6349, still in its original green livery and having already visited the 'A' shop for component recovery, awaits its short journey to the con yard and eventual cutting up in this 2 August 1971 photograph. By the end of October that same year the loco was just history.

With its overhaul and repaint complete, Hymek No. D7016 is almost ready for the road as it receives a few final adjustments outside the 'A' shop in this 2 August 1971 view. Returning to the works after being withdrawn at the end of 1974, No. D7016 joined many of its class members when, by the summer of 1975, it had become just another scrap statistic of Swindon's con yard.

With side and top panels removed, one of the short-lived BR Class 14 0-6-0 diesel hydraulic shunters, No. D9530, undergoes overhaul inside the 'A' shop alongside No. D1026 *Western Centurion* on 16 August 1971. Built during 1964/65, these Class 14 locomotives were to see more use working the industrial market after withdrawal.

Almost at the end of its overhaul and repaint, No. D3928, later to become 08760 under the BR tops system, is seen here inside the 'A' shop on 16 August 1971. Upon release from the works, this locomotive was allocated to the Southern Region Hither Green depot.

A westbound freight hauled by Warship No. D806 *Cambrian*, having just passed underneath Hay Lane bridge, approaches the eastern outskirts of Wootton Bassett on 2 October 1971. D806 had just another year to go before being withdrawn in November 1972 from Plymouth Laira depot. It was eventually sent to Swindon and met its fate with the cutter's torch during early 1975.

Not a happy sight for Class 22 followers. Withdrawn and awaiting component recovery before a meeting with the scrap man are Nos D6343, D6326, and in the distance D6307, outside the 'A' shop on 11 October 1971. No. D6307 met its end in December that year, while Nos D6343 and D6326 lasted until January and March 1972 respectively.

Approaching the site of Purton station on the then single section of track between Swindon and Kemble, two-tone green liveried Class 47 No. D1587 (later becoming 47464) has charge of the 1A19 Cheltenham to Paddington express. Taken on 1 November 1971.

On a rather gloomy winters day – 6 December 1971 – Western No. D1053 *Western Patriarch*, having just been released from the 'A' shop after its overhaul and repaint, awaits final attention before transfer back to Plymouth Laira. Meanwhile Class 08 No. D3924 stands alongside having also had attention within the works.

Arriving at Swindon in July 1971, former Ashford Class 12 shunter No. 15232 stands in Swindon's con yard awaiting scrapping together with Warship No. D847 *Strongbow* on 6 December 1971. No. 15232 would last until the following April when it too would join the long list of Swindon locomotives to receive the cutter's attention.

The early 1970s were to see withdrawn former hydraulic locomotives arriving at Swindon on an almost weekly basis. Seen here on 4 January 1972 are three withdrawn Warships awaiting their fate in the con yard. From the left are Nos D850 *Swift*, D841 *Roebuck* and D837 *Ramillies*. By June the same year these three locomotives were no more.

With the driver illuminated by the winter sun, Western No. D1072 *Western Glory* powers away from Swindon station at 11.20 am in charge of the 1C37 Paddington to Swansea express on 14 January 1972.

After being stopped by a signal check, Hymek No. D7096 makes a smoky exit from the former site of Wootton Bassett station with a westbound train of InterCity sleeper stock on 14 January 1972. This locomotive would eventually be sent to the BR technical centre at Derby after being withdrawn, being used as a dead load for research purposes.

Undergoing its last major overhaul at Swindon Works, Western No. D1000 *Western Enterprise* is almost complete in this 'A' shop view taken on 27 January 1972. Unfortunately withdrawn only two years later, this locomotive, like many of its class members, was back in the works for its destiny with the cutter's torch. By the summer of 1974 D1000 was just another pile of scrap metal.

These two Hymek locomotives have just arrived at the works after storage at Bristol Marsh Junction. In contrasting liveries, No. D7020 in original green livery accompanies blue class member No. D7042 as they await their fate at Swindon works on 27 January 1972. Both had been cut up by September the same year.

Now demolished, the former coal-fired power station at Moredon, situated to the north-west of Swindon, had in the early 1970s a small industrial rail system to cater for the trip freight coal workings from Swindon old town station. It is seen here on 26 March 1972. Andrew Barclay 0-4-0 diesel shunter No. 1197 takes a rest between shunting duties.

Entering Swindon station from the west, the Warship that became (in later years) one of Swindon works turntable celebrities was No. D818 *Glory*, seen here in normal BR service with a Bristol to Old Oak Common parcel working on 8 May 1972. Allocated to Plymouth Laira, D818 had another five months of service left before being withdrawn during the following November.

After receiving attention in Swindon works (repainted radiator grills and con rods), Newport Ebbw Junction-allocated No. D4001, still remaining in original green livery, stands next to two former Pullman driving cars, Nos W60096 and W60097, at the works reception sidings on 19 August 1972.

Almost gone! With just days lcft before it too joins its class members and becomes another statistic of the works con yard cutting crew, the remains of former Warship No. D866 *Zebra* presents a sad sight for any hydraulic fan. Photographed on 30 September 1972.

With Swindon's 'A' shop in the background, forerunner of the class of five – green liveried Ruston & Hornsby 0-6-0 locomotive PWM 650 – is engaged in shunting operations at Swindon's Newburn permanent way reclamation sidings, south of the Bristol main line, on 9 December 1972. This loco was eventually renumbered 97650 during 1979.

Again taken on 9 December 1972, with the eastern end of Swindon's 'A' shop as a backdrop, Western No. D1012 *Western Firebrand* has charge of the 1Z34 service heading towards Paddington from the west. It has just passed No. D5837 with one brake van heading in the opposite direction.

Sent to the works for scrap, former north east allocated Class 03 shunter No. 2077 seems dwarfed outside Swindon's mighty 'A' shop shortly after arrival from Thornaby depot on 14 January 1973. Withdrawn in October 1972 its days were numbered, being cut up by the end of April the same year.

Held at signals at the west end of Swindon station, No. 1683 (later to become 47485) awaits the right away with a short westbound freight on 18 February 1973.

Looking immaculate after recently being released from Swindon Works, following its mechanical overhaul and repaint Class 08 No. 3750 (later becoming 08583) awaits transfer to its allocated depot as it stands in the north sidings adjacent to Swindon station on 18 February 1973.

Heading westbound on 25 March 1973, No. D1010 *Western Campaigner* ticks over as it awaits the right away after being held by signals at Swindon station. In the distance the fuel point and depot looks busy with two Westerns, an 08 and a Class 47 all awaiting their next duty.

Approaching Swindon from the west on 9 June 1973, No. D1025 *Western Guardsman* passes under the old Midland & South Western Junction railway bridge at Rushey Platt, with the 1A71 service to Paddington. The line diverges to the left and is still in use at this time for freight traffic, being the Down main line connection leading to Swindon old town station.

Having passed the site of Wootton Bassett station and the stone terminal in the background, No. D1069 *Western Vanguard* takes the Bristol main line with the 1C77 from Paddington. Photographed on 30 June 1973.

In its final blue and grey livery, withdrawn former Western Region eight-car Pullman set Nos 60098, 60648, 60738, 60748, 60749, 60739, 60649, 60092 awaits its fate as it stands outside the works on 12 August 1973. Eventually sent to Cohen's scrap yard, in Swansea, for scrap, where by May 1974 this eight-car set was no more.

Framed by the road bridge at Hay Lane, just to the east of Wootton Bassett, No. 5630 (later becoming 31206) heads the 6B44 eastbound mixed freight towards Swindon on 13 August 1973.

Standing at Coopers' metals yard on the old Swindon to Highworth branch on 8 September 1973, is industrial locomotive No. 2, a John Fowler-built 0-4-0 of 1953, awaiting its next turn of duty. Behind are the workshop buildings of British Leyland Pressed Steel.

At a time when BR Blue was the order of the day, this 3 November 1973 image shows No. D4163 (later becoming 08933) standing outside Swindon depot in ex-works condition, and unusually painted in BR green livery, next to blue liveried No. 3607 (later becoming 08492) together with (in the background) No. 37300.

On a beautiful winter's day, and with the British Leyland Pressed Steel factory as a backdrop, No. 1603 (later becoming 47475) passes Stratton St Margaret on the approach to Swindon with the westbound 1B62 express from Paddington on the last day of the year, 31 December 1973.

With ex-carriage and wagon buildings still standing in this view, Hymek No. 7029 awaits its next duty outside Swindon depot on 7 April 1974. Today this locomotive is preserved by the Diesel Traction Group and based at the Severn Valley Railway.

Having been held at signals for a while opposite the works offices in the Up loop, Western No. D1021 *Western Cavalier* moves off and approaches Swindon station with an eastbound maroon liveried track-recording staff coach on 7 April 1974.

By 1974 Class 50s drafted in from their former Midland duties were becoming more common on the Western Region, allowing the eventual withdraw of the Class 52 Westerns. Here No. 50001 heads out of Swindon and passes underneath the former Midland & South Western Railway over bridge with the 1B86 westbound service from Paddington on 7 June 1974.

Less than two weeks after arrival from Plymouth Laira, withdrawn Western No. D1073 *Western Bulwark* stands at the rear of 'A' shop awaiting its turn for component recovery. Behind stands another withdrawn hydraulic, Hymek No. D7074, on 12 October 1974. By August the following year, D1073 was no more, becoming just another victim of the con yard scrap man.

Also taken on 12 October 1974, Warship No. D824 *Highflyer*, having arrived at Swindon for scrap from Newton Abbot, and having already been stripped of all useful components, stands at the rear of the 'A' shop as it awaits its journey and inevitable fate with the cutter's torch at the con yard. By the following June No. D824 was just a memory.

Powering the 1B50 service from Paddington, Class 50 No. 50049 (later to be named *Defiance*) speeds past the British Leyland Pressed Steel factory as it passes Stratton St Margaret on its approach to Swindon on 28 February 1975.

No. D1043 *Western Duke* awaits attention as it stands outside Swindon depot on 16 March 1975. Resident yard shunter No. 08288 can just be seen inside the building. *Western Duke* had just over another twelve months of service after this photo was taken, being withdrawn from Plymouth Laira in April 1976 and returning to Swindon the same year for component recovery. It was scrapped by February 1977.

Class 117 Bristol-based DMU set Nos B408, W51388, W59498, W51346 stand in the works reception sidings awaiting entry into the workshops for attention on 16 March 1975. Of interest also is the St Ivel milk tanker standing alongside.

After being held at signals in the Up loop outside the works, No. D1072 *Western Glory* passes Swindon depot and approaches the station with the 8A39 eastbound freight on 17 March 1975. D1072 was one of the latter batches of Westerns to be withdrawn, surviving until November 1976.

With the town skyline and works visible in the background, Class 50 No. 50014 heads out of Swindon and passes the allotments opposite Rushey Platt junction, as it heads west with the 1B70 express from Paddington on 26 April 1975.

Travelling on the then single track section between Swindon and Kemble, and having just passed the remains of Purton station in the far distance, Class 47 No. 47137 has charge of the 1B04 16.48 Paddington to Cheltenham Spa service as it approaches Purton Common level crossing on 20 May 1975.

Situated on the Gloucester line and with the now-demolished Moredon power station in the background, Class 25 No. 25172, and its train of dogfish wagons, is engaged in ballast duties alongside the former Bremell sidings fuel depot between Swindon and Purton on 8 June 1975.

One of the lucky Westerns to survive into preservation, and a locomotive that I was personally involved with regarding its restoration and repaint back into maroon livery. No. D1062 *Western Courier*, purchased by the Western Locomotive Association, stands adjacent to the main works turntable as it awaits its long overhaul and eventual entry back into service on 9 August 1975.

The first tour on the Western Region to feature a Deltic locomotive was on 12 October 1975, organised by BR and utilising No. 55003 *Meld.* The special ran from Paddington to Cardiff. Seen here at Swindon station on the return journey, *Meld* is held at signals while No. D1065 *Western Consort* approaches with a westbound express from Paddington.

Looking in good external condition, No. D1013 *Western Ranger* soaks up the afternoon sun outside Swindon depot on 12 November 1975. Today this locomotive is one of the lucky survivors being preserved by the Western Locomotive Association based on the Severn Valley Railway.

Withdrawn the previous October from Plymouth Laira, No. D1059 *Western Empire* is seen in Swindon's 'A' shop awaiting component recovery on 1 January 1976. By the end of July the same year, D1059 was reduced to just scrap metal.

Standing in the works reception sidings adjacent to the Gloucester line on 2 May 1976, having arrived from Plymouth Laira the day before, three withdrawn Westerns, Nos D1040 *Western Queen*, D1047 *Western Lord* and D1046 *Western Marquis*, await their short journey to the 'A' shop for component recovery. By November the same year these three locomotives had been scrapped.

It wasn't just hydraulics being scrapped in Swindon's con yard during the 1970s. Never to see service again and with engine and other components removed, the remains of former Crewe-based Class 24 No. 24145 presents a sorry site as it meets the end of its life as recorded here on 9 May 1976.

Photographed at the far western end of the con yard and with 'C' shop's giant crane as a backdrop, it seems as though nature is taking over the site. No. D1006 *Western Stalwart* keeps company with classmate No. D1031 *Western Rifleman* as they await their turn for the cutter's torch on 9 May 1976.

Seen here passing over the Wootton Bassett road bridge to the far west of Swindon, No. D1070 *Western Gauntlet* approaches the site of Rushey Platt junction as it heads west with four parcel vans on 19 July 1976.

After being held at signals in the Up loop just outside the works, No. D1005 *Western Venturer* moves away with an eastbound train of empty coal wagons on 10 August 1976.

Held in the Up loop to the east of Swindon at Stratton St Margaret, No. D1041 *Western Prince* ticks over as it awaits its path onto the main line at the head of a rather long eastbound mixed freight on 21 September 1976. One of the last Westerns to be withdrawn, in February 1977, *Western Prince* is now preserved on the East Lancs Railway.

After being stored at Crewe for nearly twelve months, former Class 24 No. 24055 was sent to Swindon in September 1976 for eventual scrapping. Seen here outside the 'A' shop on 24 October 1976, the loco awaits its turn for component recovery before its last journey to the con yard. By the end of the year the loco was no more.

Again after a period of storage at Crewe, these three former Class 24s were sent to Swindon for scrapping. Still in green livery Nos 24092 and 24136 keep company with blue livery No. 24060, as they await their fate in the sidings to the rear of the 'A' shop on 24 October 1976. All had gone by the end of January 1977.

Scenes such as this were all too common within the confines of Swindon's con yard during the 1970s. Surrounded by the remnants of other scrapped locomotives, the remains of former No. D1046 *Western Marquis* has not long to go when this photo was taken on 24 October 1976.

In the bay at Swindon station stands the local DMU service to Gloucester, while Class 50 No. 50022 (later to be named *Anson*) has charge of the 12.35 service to Bristol Temple Meads when captured on this cold and frosty day on 4 December 1976.

With the demise of the class imminent, Western Hydraulic railtours were hitting fever pitch in early 1977. Seen here on 13 February that year, No. D1010 *Western Campaigner* pulls away from Swindon station with the Railway Pictorial Publications organised 'Western Requim' railtour, en route from Paddington to the South Wales Valleys, via the Gloucester line.

This sight could be mistaken for the 1960s, but it is in fact 5 March 1977, where, alongside the former works test house, preserved Warship No. D821 *Greyhound* undergoes a repaint back into maroon livery.

A hydraulic view around the works turntable on 5 March 1977. Withdrawn Western No. D1005 *Western Venturer* awaits its 'A' shop visit for component recovery while ill-fated Warship No. D818 *Glory* keeps company with preserved Hymek No. D7029.

Here we see two Westerns that escaped the dreaded con yard visit, photographed inside the former works weighbridge building on 5 March 1977. On the left stands preserved No. D1062 *Western Courier* undergoing work to the roof hatches, while fellow preserved example No. D1023 *Western Fusilier* stands to the right.

The great cavernous roof of the 'A' shop dwarfs the two shunters in this view taken on 24 March 1977. To the left with its engine removed, and still in green livery, stands former Taunton Fairwater yard departmental shunter PWM 652, while to the right is No. 08117 in the works for conversion to an independent snowplough.

Standing on the centre traverser in this 'A' shop view, again taken on 24 March 1977, withdrawn Class 24 No. 24025 gets ready to be released onto its allocated road for partial dismantling before its journey to the con yard. Arriving at Swindon works from storage at Crewe during January 1977, by the end of July nothing remained of this former midland locomotive.

Back to maroon livery the locomotive which I personally had an involvement in the repaint of. No. D1062 *Western Courier*, preserved by the Western Locomotive Association, awaits the application of yellow to be applied to the front panel, while undergoing an engine test outside the works weighbridge on 23 April 1977.

With restoration almost complete back to its original green livery, the diesel traction group's Hymek No. D7029 awaits its numbers to be applied as it keeps company with Warship No. D818 *Glory* around the works turntable on 23 April 1977.

Withdrawn in January 1976 after collision damage, No. 24089 arrived at Swindon works the following December. Here this former midland locomotive, already having its engine and other useful components removed, awaits its inevitable fate as it stands outside the 'A' shop on 30 April 1977.

A photo that says it all, with 'The End' painted on the side of No. D1028 *Western Hussar* this once proud locomotive of the Western fleet heads a line-up of former class members, Nos D1057 *Western Chieftan*, D1064 *Western Regent*, D1025 *Western Guardsman* and D1012 *Western Firebrand* all stand at the rear of the 'A' shop on 30 April 1977.

Introduced at the start of the October timetable in 1976, HST sets began operating between Paddington, Bristol and South Wales. Recorded here on 7 May 1977, set No. 253019 passes the works during the BR Organised Commemorative 'Silver Jubilee' speed record attempt from Bristol Temple Meads to Paddington.

The late 1970s Swindon works began being involved in Southern Region DEMU work. Having received mechanical attention and a complete repaint, Class 207 three-car set No. 1301 stands in ex-works condition in the works reception sidings, as it awaits transfer back to the Southern Region on 7 May 1977.

Normally on a visit to see what was on Swindon shed there would be at least one Class 08 outside, on 7 May 1977 it was a case of three for the price of one. Nos 08583, 08140 and 08804 soak up the spring sunshine as they await their next duty.

It was quite a rare event to see ex BR-locomotives at the works. Photographed on 21 May 1977, former Goole-allocated Class 04 No. D2267 was, in 1970, sold for further industrial use to the Ford Motor Co. at Dagenham, where it received its new identity of No. 6. Its first visit to the works for mechanical attention though was not without incident, as unfortunately No. 6 has managed to become derailed prior to entering the 'A' shop.

While locomotives were generally disposed of in the yard, the corrugated structure of 'C' shop in the distance mainly concentrated on redundant wagon stock. On 21 May 1977 Western No. D1065 *Western Consort* stands alongside the overhead gantry and awaits final cutting up.

Entering Swindon off the Gloucester line with a Cheltenham to Paddington service, No. 50021 (later to be named *Rodney*) passes the small one road depot, while Class 47 No. 47031 awaits its next duty on 27 May 1977.

On 27 May 1977, following its complete restoration to running order by the Western Locomotive Association, and looking immaculate in its new coat of maroon livery, No. D1062 *Western Courier* is seen here being hauled out of the works by resident Swindon Class 08 No. 08288 for its short trip to the transfer yard, and eventual onward movement to the Dart Valley Railway at Paignton.

Approaching the Hay Lane road bridge just to the east of Wootton Bassett, Class 31 No. 31257 has charge of a rather mixed assortment of stock as it powers the afternoon Bristol to Paddington parcel service on 27 May 1977.

Also approaching Hay Lane road bridge on the same day, 27 May 1977, although this time looking eastwards towards Swindon. Class 50 No. 50004 (later to be named *St Vincent*) heads west towards Wootton Bassett with a short engineers' train from Swindon yard.

Standing in the works reception sidings, having undergone a mechanical overhaul and repaint, Southern DEMU No. 1101 (later renumbered 205001) awaits transfer back to its home depot, as it stands alongside former condemned Eastern Region buffet coach No. E9129E on 18 September 1977.

With 1977 being the occasion of the Queen's Silver Jubilee, Swindon Works marked the celebrations with an appropriate Crown motif on the side of the DMU repair shops, situated alongside the Bristol main line. Photographed on the morning of 18 September 1977, ex-works Class 119 set B575 Nos W51060, W59419, and W510088, together with Class 120 No. M50669, await final attention before onward movement back to their respective depots.

Organised by the Oxford Publishing Company, a Class 45 railtour 'Ebbw Vale Rambler' was run between Oxford and some of the freight-only lines in South Wales on 18 September 1977. Seen here hauled by No. 45055 *Royal Corps of Transport* the special passes Swindon Works on its outward run.

One of BR Western Region's celebrity named locomotives, Class 47 No. 47079 *George Jackson Churchward*, has charge of a Paddington to Bristol parcel service as it makes a short stop at Swindon station on 28 September 1977.

How the mighty fall! All that remains of two former Western hydraulics, and with only the cabs for identification, No. D1001 *Western Pathfinder* and No. D1065 *Western Consort* are reduced to scrap metal as they litter the con yard site at Swindon Works on 4 March 1978.

Approaching the site of Purton station on the singe line section between Kemble and Swindon, Bristol-based Class 119 DMU set No. B585, W51075, W59434, W51103 is photographed heading the 11.32 am Cheltenham Spa to Swindon service on 26 March 1978.

Approaching Gypsy Lane road bridge, resident Swindon-based Class 08 No. 08839 has charge of a rake of sheeted steel wagons as it heads up the last remaining section of the old Highworh branch line to the British Leyland Pressed Steel Co. sidings on 7 April 1978. Another rail user at this time, Coopers Scrap metal reprocessing plant can be seen in the background.

Another image of the old Highworth branch is seen here as one of the British Leyland Fowler 0-4-0 industrial locomotives, No. 422009, enters the exchange sidings from the pressed steel plant on 7 April 1978. In the distance can be seen No. 08839.

Passing Swindon Works on 15 April 1978, and with a coating of stone dust covering the cabs and roof hatches, Class 37s Nos 37296 and 37292 head west at the head of an Amey Roadstone aggregate service, en route back to Merehead Quarry in Somerset.

With a healthy compliment of assorted wagons in Swindon's transfer yard, these two Class 25s create a scene more reminiscent of a Midlands goods yard rather than Swindon. Class 25s Nos 25270 and 25260 back onto the 15.20 Swindon to Bescot freight service on 17 April 1978.

With Swindon's resident Class 08 shunter No. 08804 outside the maintenance shed, Class 47 No. 47142, having passed the works approaches the station with a block oil train from Milford Haven, heads eastwards on 3 May 1978.

Prototype HST power car No. 43001, after being held at signals, departs Swindon station and heads westwards with a short, unidentified test train service from Paddington, comprising an unidentified train recording coach together with passenger coach No. 41000 at the rear on 12 May 1978. Fortunately, HST power car 43001 is now preserved as part of the National Collection.

With the main administration offices forming a backdrop to this photo, the works reception sidings often held something of interest, either recent ex-works rolling stock or something that had arrived overnight to be admitted for attention. On 19 May 1978 it was the turn of the BR Ultrasonic Test Train to take my interest comprising vehicles No. DB 975008 (formerly E79612) and No. DB 975007 (formerly E79018).

Heading the 7.54 am Weston-super-Mare to Paddington service, HST set No. 253015 passes Swindon station on the centre road, while Stratford depot silver roof Class 47 No. 47167 waits for the right away with an unidentified eastbound service on 27 May 1978. No. 47167 was later renumbered as No. 47580 and gained the name *County of Essex* the following year.

Named the month before, Class 50 No. 50012 *Benbow* stands outside Swindon shed on 28 May 1978, while resident Swindon-based Class 08s Nos 08839 and 08411 are in the distance. Unfortunately, No. 50012 was not one of the lucky Class 50s to survive, having another eleven years' service left before meeting its end at Vic Berry's Leicester scrap yard in 1989.

Stratton St Margaret, on the eastern outskirts of Swindon, forms the setting to this scene. Named only two months previously, Class 50 No. 50019 *Ramillies* has charge of the 8.31 Cheltenham to Paddington service, running 20 minutes late on 3 June 1978.

A mix of traction in this view seen in the con yard on 16 July 1978. Stripped of all useful components Class 125 DMU No. E51165 keeps company with withdrawn Westerns Nos D1022 *Western Sentinel*, D1011 *Western Thunderer*, D1034 *Western Dragoon* and D1021 *Western Cavalier*. To the far left can be seen another locomotive line-up headed by No. 24084.

Swindon's transfer goods yard could always come up with a few surprises. A definite Southern scene was recorded on 4 September 1978. Withdrawn from Ashford depot, three former Class 71s Nos 71002, 71008 and 71007 arrived on an overnight freight on their last ever journey to Cashmoor's scrap yard in Newport.

After a brief signal check, Class 45 No. 45045 *Coldstream Guardsman* pulls away from Swindon station with the 14.30 mixed freight from Swindon's transfer goods yard to Gloucester and the Midlands on 9 November 1978.

With the works 'A' shop as a good backdrop, together with the branch to Swindon's old town at Rushey Platt junction now taken out of use. On 25 November 1978 Railway Pictorial Publications organised the 'Welsh Wonder No. 1' railtour from Paddington to Cardiff and the Welsh Valleys. Here we see Nos 46001, 25157 and 25225 making a smoky exit from the town on their outward run to South Wales.

Swindon-built Class 123 DMU power cars Nos E52103 and E52095, are seen here ex-works and fresh from the paint shop as they stand alongside the Bristol main line on 12 May 1979. Although initially working the Portsmouth to Cardiff route when introduced in 1963, they were by now awaiting their onward movement to Hull depot and their working of the Trans Pennine services.

With its bogies removed and being positioned on jacks, Metro-Cammell built and Eastern Region allocated Class 101 DMU power car No. E51500 receives attention in the DMU repair shops on 19 May 1979.

Swindon Works open days were always well attended, not just by enthusiasts but the workforce and their families too. 1970s fashion is in abundance in this view taken during the open day on 19 May 1979. Preserved Western No. D1041 *Western Prince* stands outside the 'A' shop generating plenty of interest with its cab visits, together with Class 08s and Southern EMUs seen in the distance.

A trio of Class 37s grace the depot sidings in this view taken on 15 September 1979. Nos 37292, 37225 and 37302 are accompanied by ex-works Class 08 No. 08501. In the distance the rear power car of HST No. 43014 enters the station with the 14.38 Weston-super-Mare to Paddington service.

Because of locomotive problems encountered with the original 'East Anglian' railtour of 27 January 1979, F&W Railtours organised the 'East Anglian re-run' tour from Worcester to Norwich and Lowestoft on 29 September 1979. Class 40 No. 40006 was the motive power on this occasion, and (in excellent external condition) heads the special past the British Leyland factory as it approaches Stratton St Margaret on its outward run.

A locomotive which narrowly escaped a visit to the con yard and the cutter's torch, No. D1015 *Western Champion*, safely preserved and in the hands of the Diesel Traction Group, undergoes restoration outside the works weighbridge building on 13 January 1980.

With the destination blind reading Aylesbury, London-based Class 121 single-car DMU L122 No. 55022 awaits the fitters' attention as it stands on jacks inside the DMU repair shops on 13 January 1980.

A scene perhaps more reminiscent of Eastleigh workshops rather than Swindon. Southern Region narrow-bodied Hastings line Class 201 DEMU No. 1007 also stands on jacks in the DMU repair shops as it undergoes mechanical attention, before moving onto the paint shop on 13 January 1980.

Powering the 8.31 am Cheltenham Spa to Paddington service on 10 May 1980, Class 50 No. 50025 *Invincible* passes Moredon as it approaches the northern outskirts of Swindon. The line to the right is the extended siding leading to the Bremell oil depot just out of view in the distance behind the road bridge.

One week later on 17 May 1980, again it was a Class 50 in charge of the 8.31 am Cheltenham Spa to Paddington service, photographed here at Stratton St Margaret. No. 50007 *Hercules* was the chosen loco. This locomotive achieved celebrity status when in February 1984 it was named *Sir Edward Elgar* and painted in Great Western lined green livery.

Purchased for preservation, following a long period of storage at Newton Abbot, Western No. D1041 *Western Prince* was sent to Swindon Works for mechanical attention and repainting before moving onto Horwich Works for the open day there, and eventually its new home and base at the East Lancs Railway at Bury. Recorded here on 17 May 1980, No. D1041 stands outside the works alongside the Bristol main line as it awaits its journey north.

An unusual visitor to the 'A' shop, photographed on 10 August 1980, was former Tinsley depot master and slave hump shunter No. 13003. With wheels and rods removed, 13003 (formerly No. D4188) awaits attention as it stands next to No. 08093. This loco had another five years' life left working in Yorkshire before being withdrawn in 1985.

After receiving collision damage at Stonebridge Park in London, following a shunting incident in March 1980, No. 25218 was sent to Swindon Works for repairs. Seen here outside the former test house, No. 25218 is almost set for the road again after its visit to the 'A' shop and a fresh application of yellow on the cab front. Keeping company with the Class 25, departmental shunter No. PWM 97652 awaits its turn for attention on 10 August 1980.

Withdrawn way back in 1968, the former Class 28 No. D5705 was transferred to departmental stock as a train heating unit, being used at various locations around the Western Region and obtaining the number TDB 968006. Following a period out of use at Bristol Bath Rd for many months, it was eventually moved to Swindon in June 1980 for storage and asbestos removal. Photographed here in the general stores yard on 22 August 1980, No. TDB 968006 still retains its original BR green livery as it awaits its future. Happily, the future was secure for this loco as eventually it was purchased by the diesel traction group.

Held at signals in the Up loop outside the works main offices on 24 September 1980, Class 31s Nos 31117 and 31265 await the right away with an eastbound freight composed mostly of loaded coal wagons.

Sent to Swindon for storage from Plymouth Laira, these four Class 46s were unusually positioned in the Down sidings opposite the works, rather than the usual locomotive reception sidings by the Gloucester line. Nos 46027, 46026, 46028 and 46025 await the decision as to their future on 4 October 1980. Happily for these locomotives, their wait wasn't too long at Swindon with all four being transferred to Gateshead depot by the following November.

The Kent coast EMU refurbishment programme was a major contract for the works in the late 1970s/early 1980s with the complete rebuilding of the 4-CEP Class 411 fleet. Outside the 'A' shop on 5 October 1980, driving trailers from sets Nos 7210 and 7130 await further attention after all internal fittings have been removed.

Situated to the west of the Gloucester main line, the works north yard became, in the 1980s, a dumping ground for either stored or withdrawn locomotives. Viewed here on 24 October 1980, two of Healey Mills depot's withdrawn Class 40s, Nos 40156 and 40071, stand alongside another row of locomotives headed by Class 08 No. 08453.

A sight many travellers would see as they sped their way on the main line from Paddington to Bristol or South Wales. Withdrawn and redundant locomotives were appearing all over the place. This line up, captured outside the works weighbridge building on 2 November 1980, records Nos 25001, 25013, 25021, 25019, preserved Western No. D1015 *Western Champion*, No. 08128 and No. 40156.

With engines removed and stripped of useful components, the body shells of two former main line locomotives await the cutter's torch at the rear of the 'A' shop on 2 November 1980. Class 40 No. 40108, a former Longsight Manchester loco, keeps company with former Bristol Bath Rd-allocated No. 31136. By the year end both locomotives were just a pile of scrap metal.

Following accident damage to the front of the cab, sustained during a collision to the east of Swindon at Uffington, silver roof example and Stratford depot-allocated Class 47 No. 47566 awaits assessment as it soaks up the morning winter sun outside Swindon depot on 5 December 1980.

HST set No. 253029 comprising power cars No. 43127 on the front, together with No. 43128 at the rear, depart Swindon station at 12.06 pm with the 11.20 am Paddington to Paignton service on a perfect winter's day, 3 January 1981.

With storm clouds fast approaching and the 'A' shop in the background the vast size of these workshops can be appreciated. Awaiting their turn for attention in the works on 4 January 1981 are Class 08s Nos 08015 and 08059, together with one of the Kent coast EMUs for refurbishment, No. 7196.

The works pattern store makes for a good backdrop in this view as withdrawn Class 03 No. 03080, having visited the 'A' shop for all reusable components to be removed, stands as just a shell alongside the main works turntable. It is awaiting its short journey to the con yard and eventual cutting up on 22 March 1981.

Looking pristine and back in its original BR green livery, a loco which many thought was safe at the time, former Warship No. D818 *Glory*, looks the part as it stands on display alongside the main works turntable on 22 March 1981. Preservation wasn't to be for this locomotive though. It was only four years later when, in the last week of October 1985, No. D818 was hauled to the rear of the 'A' shop and there reduced to scrap metal.

HST set No. 253007, with power cars No. 43015 on the front together with No. 43014 on the rear, passes Swindon Works on 28 March 1981 in charge of the 7.52 am Weston-super-Mare to Paddington service.

The former 'C' shop looms large in this image, as viewed through the con yard undergrowth and surrounded by redundant wagon stock. The shell of former Class 25 No. 25074 stands alone as it awaits its turn to be cut up on 17 April 1981.

Having recently arrived at the works a few days previously, two former Class 40s, Nos 40161 together with fellow classmate No. 40137 behind, stand alongside the weighbridge building and await their fate on 17 April 1981. In the distance can be seen an unrecorded ex-works Class 08. By year end both Class 40s had been reduced to scrap metal.

A view outside the 'A' shop again on 17 April 1981, two stored Class 31s, Nos 31-274 and 31264, stand alongside withdrawn Class 25 No. 25010. While the two Class 31s were to see service again, No. 25010 was not so lucky; by June the same year the loco was cut up in the con yard.

Standing alongside the Bristol main line on 24 May 1981, this line up of stored and withdrawn locomotives present an interesting sight outside the works, being positioned as they are to act as a barrier for visitors during the forthcoming 6 June open day. The locomotives are Nos 31004, 31269, 25293, 25166, 25070 and 25263.

Refurbished in its new DMU off-white and rail blue livery, Class 101 No. W51517, from Bristol set No. B801, stands to the rear of the 'A' shop awaiting further attention on 18 October 1981.

Photographed on 13 December 1981 in Swindon's Up yard, just east of the station, these four withdrawn locomotives stand in the Wiltshire snow and await entry into the works having just arrived overnight from the Midlands. No. 40134 heads the line-up together with Nos 40095, 25292 and 40178.

It was nice to see Class 40s actually in traffic rather than for scrap at Swindon. Heading the return leg of the 'Cotswold Venturer' railtour, organised by S.V.R. Railtours, from Paddington back to York, Nos 40057 and 40084 head out of Swindon on the Gloucester line past Barnfield Rd on 8 May 1982.

By 1982 Swindon's north yard alongside the Gloucester line was overflowing with withdrawn and stored locomotives, as this photo illustrates. Heading this line-up, taken on 23 May 1982, and viewed from left to right are Nos 08578, 45018, 45071, 08495, 25081, 08869, 08717 and 08279.

Passing the parcel sidings just east of the station, Class 50 No. 50004 *St Vincent* approaches with the 8.24 Cheltenham Spa to Paddington service on 29 May 1982. Ten more years were left for this locomotive. When taken to C.F. Booth's scrap yard at Rotherham, No. 50004 was reduced to scrap metal during May 1992.

After complete refurbishment in the works. Class 411 EMU No. 1577 (formerly No. 7166) awaits its journey back to the Southern Region as it stands in the reception sidings adjacent to the works main offices on 29 May 1982.

Photographed in the works north yard after visiting the 'A' shop and being stripped of engines and other components, two former Class 40s, Nos 40036 and 40010, *Empress of Britain*, await their short journey and appointment with the con yard cutting crew on 18 July 1982. No. 40036 was gone by October the same year while No. 40010 lasted until August 1983.

Former Birkenhead docks Class 03 No. 03196, unofficially named *Joyce*, stands outside Swindon depot after recently being released from works after overhaul. Keeping company with No. 03196 is resident Swindon shunter No. 08487 on 18 September 1982.

Passing the station en route from Strawberry Hill depot, London, to the works reception sidings, Class 33 No. 33064 brings in Southern Class 411 EMUs 1552 (back again for attention after only being released ex-works the previous month), together with unrefurbished set No. 7017, on 3 March 1983.

Standing outside the works after overhaul and fresh from the paint shop, one of only ten Class 128 motor parcel vans, No. W55992, awaits final inspection before returning to its home depot of Reading on 2 July 1983.

Photographed on 13 August 1983, withdrawn two-car Class 414 EMU No. 6123 stands at the reception sidings, alongside the works main offices, having recently arrived from Ramsgate depot for asbestos removal and eventual cutting up.

Awaiting their next call of duty outside Swindon shed, a pair of Class 31s, Nos 31300 and 31177, share their time with freshly repainted and ex-works Class 08 No. 08795 on 14 August 1983.

Following Doncaster works heavy workload, during the late 1983 early 1984 period, a handful of Class 31s and Class 37s were transferred to Swindon for attention. Seen here surrounded by Class 08 radiator fronts, No. 37213 receives attention inside the 'A' shop on 12 May 1984.

In April 1984, following an unprecedented move, three former Scottish Class 27s Nos 27019, 27036 and 27002 arrived at the works for a decision on their future and possible repair. Making a view more akin to Glasgow rather than Swindon, these three locos stand at the rear of 'A' shop on 12 May 1984.

Its refurbishment almost complete, former Scottish Region-allocated Class 08 No. 08710 awaits the works painters to apply the black chevrons on the cab end in this 'A' shop view taken on 12 May 1984.

A flashback to the 1960s in this view, only it's 1984. Standing around the works main turntable are preserved Western No. D1015 *Western Champion*, back in desert sand livery, alongside Warship No. D818 *Glory* again taken on 12 May 1984.

Presenting an unusual sight outside the former DMU workshops and showing off its new Scottish Strathclyde PTE colours, the first DMU set to receive this livery after refurbishment at Swindon works was unit 101340, comprising Nos Sc51990, Sc59802 and Sc51803, recorded here on 20 August 1984.

Other than on railtour duties or when stored at the works after being withdrawn, Class 20s were rare at Swindon making this photograph taken on 23 August 1984, of No. 20192 parked at the depot sidings, an interesting image; particularly when an unidentified InterCity HST set is also on shed and receiving attention in the background.

Another unusual locomotive seen at Swindon, former Class 25 No. 25310, seen here in its departmental role as mobile heating unit No. 97250 *Ethel 1*, is captured in the works reception sidings awaiting haulage back to Eastfield depot in Glasgow after undergoing attention in the works on 18 October 1984.

Awaiting movement back to their respective depots after repair and being released from the works, these five Class 08s Nos 08730, 08910, 08690, 08668, and 08676 stand in Swindon's transfer yard sidings on 18 October 1984.

The signal gantry, to the east of Swindon station, frames Class 47 No. 47235 as it heads east with oil tanks from Milford Haven. Alongside and having arrived off the Gloucester line, Class 45 No. 45112 *The Royal Army Ordnance Corps* reverses back to the station with its train of parcel vans on 28 June 1985.

In its special Great Western green livery, celebrity Class 47 No. 47484 *Isambard Kingdom Brunel*, together with two chocolate and cream liveried coaches Nos 4593 and 35128, wait at Swindon station for a returning steam special from Gloucester before returning to Old Oak Common with empty stock on 7 August 1985.

Held at signals in the Up loop opposite the works, en route from Bristol Marsh Junction to Old Oak Common, two HST InterCity 125 power cars (in different liveries) make for an interesting comparison. No. 43031, in its new livery together with No. 43035, in the original blue and yellow, are photographed on 11 August 1985.

With its distinctive red dragon logo on the front, Class 116 Cardiff-based DMU set No. C305, Nos W53131, W59039 and W53089 are photographed passing Barnfield Rd on the northern outskirts of town with the 15.28 pm Swindon to Gloucester service on 11 August 1985.

Re-engined as a testbed for the proposed Class 58 locomotives, the unique Class 47 No. 47901 pulls away from a signal check at Swindon station. It is heading a westbound train of empty Yeoman stone hoppers bound for Westbury yard on 27 September 1985.

Not normally what you would expect to see at Swindon works. Former Waterloo & City Underground car No. S73 was dispatched to the works for asbestos removal and complete overhaul. Seen here not long after arrival and with two barrier wagons at either end, it awaits its turn in the 'A' shop on 6 October 1985.

Having travelled down from Allerton depot, Liverpool, with a destination blind reading Wigan, Class 108 DMU Nos M54494, M51416 pull away from the station following a signal check en route to the works reception sidings on 29 October 1985.

Purchased for use on the Mid Hants Railway, Inverness-based Class 27 No. 27007 was sent to Swindon works for remedial attention before continuing on to Hampshire. Seen here in the works reception sidings not long after arrival, this former Scottish-based locomotive presents an unusual site as it awaits its turn in the 'A' shop on 31 October 1985.

As part of the GWR 150 celebrations during 1985, Bristol Bath Rd-allocated Class 117 DMU set No. B430, Nos W51410, W59520, W51368, was given a special GWR chocolate and cream livery. Photographed here on 5 April 1986, B430 is seen stabled in the sidings adjacent to Swindon station.

Held at signals in the Up loop outside the works, the driver is on the phone to Swindon signal box as Class 37 No. 37206 has charge of a short eastbound engineers service on 4 May 1986.

With a mix of old and new InterCity 125 liveries, HST set No. 253034, with power car No. 43138 leading, departs Swindon station at 19.46 pm and catches the evening sun after a day of heavy showers with the 18.45 Paddington to Cardiff service, on 17 June 1987.

Again, photographed in the late evening summer sun and with the station in the distance, large logo Class 56 No. 56048 prepares to move onto Swindon depot on 3 August 1987.

Passing the British Leyland factory at Stratton St Margaret, re-liveried HST InterCity 125 power car No. 43124 *B.B.C. Points West*, together with No. 43185 on the rear, approach Swindon with the 12.00 Paddington to Swansea service on 6 August 1987.

After reversal in Swindon's cocklebury yard, Yeoman-liveried Class 59 No. 59001 *Yeoman Endeavour* passes the station and heads west with a Merehead to Wootton Bassett aggregate working on 26 August 1987.

Looking immaculate in its recent Railfreight red stripe livery, Class 56 No. 56049 is brought to a stand by signals in the Up loop outside the works as it heads eastbound with a train of ARC stone hoppers on 27 August 1987.

Petroleum sector livery Class 56 No. 56001 *Whatley* pulls away from a signal check at Swindon station and heads west with its train of oil tanks bound for South Wales on 15 March 1988.

With all three engines ticking over, Class 37 No. 37229 *The Cardiff Rod Mill* and No. 37239, together with Class 50 No. 50031 *Hood*, are held in the Up loop outside the works main offices heading east on 16 March 1988.

Celebrity BR green livery Class 33 No. 33008 *Eastleigh* passes Swindon station as it heads west with a short train of ballast wagons from the transfer yard on 30 March 1988.

A view of the Up main line looking east from Swindon station, having brought a freight service into the Up sidings seen in the distance. Class 47 No. 47540 (renumbered from 47132) prepares to go onto the depot on 28 April 1988.

With its number 207 painted on the cab front, Class 47 No. 47207 *Bulmers of Hereford* heads past Barnfield Rd on the Gloucester line as it heads the British Leyland Swindon to Birmingham Longbridge car components train. Photographed on 23 May 1988.

After bringing in the 18.07 pm service from Paddington, Class 47 No. 47589 (renumbered from 47251) pauses at Swindon station on 7 June 1988. The original Great Western Up side building was still very much in use, contrasting with the modern office block on the Down side.

A view from Swindon station foot bridge, looking east on 6 July 1988, features large logo Class 47 No. 47634 *Henry Ford* (renumbered from 47158) entering with the 18.07 pm service from Paddington. In the distance can be seen an unidentified InterCity Class 47 together with one van in the parcel bay.

In charge of the afternoon Bristol to Old Oak Common vans, InterCity liveried Class 47 No. 47501 *Craftsman* is held at signals in the Up loop outside the works as it awaits its path eastwards on 16 September 1988.

A livery which was a favourite of many Class 50 followers, and making a fine locomotive study, is large logo example No. 50036 *Victorious*, seen here as it awaits its next turn of duty in the sidings outside Swindon depot on 21 June 1989. Withdrawn from Laira depot less than two years after this photo was taken, No. 50036 met her end at C.F. Boots Rotherham scrap yard during the summer of 1992.

In revised InterCity livery, H.S.T. Set 253-045 comprising power cars 43171 on the front and 43137 at the rear, pass Stratton St Margaret on the approach to Swindon with the 19.00 pm service from Paddington to Swansea on 3 July 1989.